PASCHAL GREYSTONE

The 31-Day Car Sales Challenge

Transform Your Sales Skills

First published by PC PASCHAL CREATION PUBLICATION 2024

Copyright © 2024 by PASCHAL GREYSTONE

All rights reserved. No part of this publication may be reproduced, stored or transmitted in any form or by any means, electronic, mechanical, photocopying, recording, scanning, or otherwise without written permission from the publisher. It is illegal to copy this book, post it to a website, or distribute it by any other means without permission.

Review

"The 31-Day Car Sales Challenge: Transform Your Sales Skills" is a masterful guide that takes sales professionals on an intensive journey to elevate their skills and performance. With a well-structured 31-day plan, the book covers essential aspects of car sales, from developing a growth mindset to mastering advanced techniques. The practical exercises, actionable strategies, and insightful tips make it an invaluable resource for anyone looking to enhance their sales abilities. Whether you're a seasoned professional or just starting in the industry, this book provides the tools and motivation needed to achieve lasting success. A must-read for those committed to excelling in the competitive world of car sales."

First edition

This book was professionally typeset on Reedsy.
Find out more at reedsy.com

Contents

I   Dedication

The Road Ahead	3
Purpose and Goals	3
What to Expect	4
Day-by-Day Structure	4
Daily Challenges	5
The Journey Towards Mastery	6
Commitment to Success	7
Part 1: Laying the Foundation	8
Day 1: Mindset Matters	8
Day 2: Know Your Product Inside Out	10
Day 3: Understanding the Buyer	12
Day 4: Setting Daily Goals	15
Day 5: Effective Communication	16
Day 6: Overcoming Objections	19
Day 7: Mastering Time Management	22
Part 2: Sharpening Your Skills	25
Day 8: Mastering the Test Drive	25
Day 9: The Art of Negotiation	28
Day 10: Building a Referral Network	30
Day 11: Time Management for Sales Success	32
Day 12: Leveraging Social Media	35
Day 13: Perfecting Your Follow-Up	37

Day 14: Closing the Deal	39
Part 3: Advanced Techniques	43
Day 15: The Psychology of Selling	43
Day 16: Handling Difficult Customers	45
Day 17: The Power of Storytelling	47
Day 18: Creating a Winning Sales Presentation	50
Day 19: Personal Development for Sales Success	52
Day 20: Ethical Selling	54
Day 21: Analyzing Your Sales Performance	56
Day 22: Advanced Negotiation Techniques	58
Part 4: Mastery and Beyond	62
Day 23: Building Long-Term Relationships	62
Day 24: Adapting to Market Changes	63
Day 25: Leadership in Sales	65
Day 26: Leveraging Technology	66
Day 27: The Importance of Networking	67
Day 28: Financial Literacy for Sales Professionals	68
Day 29: Developing a Personal Sales Brand	69
Day 30: Scaling Your Sales Efforts	71
Day 31: Celebrating Success and Setting Future Goals	72
Embracing the Journey of Mastery	74
The Journey Continues	76
Encouraging Readers to Keep Applying the Skills Learned	76
Motivating the Reader to Pursue Excellence in Their Sales Career	77
Appendix: Tools and Resources for Sales Professionals	80
List of Recommended Books, Websites, and Tools for Further Learning	80
Templates and Worksheets for Daily Sales Activities	84

Dedication

To all the dedicated sales professionals who strive every day to excel in their craft, this book is for you. Your commitment to mastering the art of sales, your drive to continuously improve, and your unwavering passion for helping customers find the perfect vehicle inspire this guide. May this book serve as a valuable tool on your journey to becoming a top performer in the car sales industry. Here's to your continued success and growth.

The Road Ahead

Purpose and Goals

The automotive industry is one of the most competitive markets, with thousands of sales professionals striving to capture the attention and trust of potential buyers. As the industry evolves, so must the skills and strategies of those working within it. The purpose of **The 31-Day Car Sales Challenge: Transform Your Sales Skills** is to equip you with the tools, techniques, and mindset needed to excel in this fast-paced environment.

This book is more than just a guide—it is a comprehensive roadmap designed to help you elevate your sales performance to new heights in just 31 days. Whether you are a seasoned professional seeking to refine your approach or a newcomer eager to make a mark, this book will provide you with the insights and strategies necessary to thrive.

The ultimate goal of this challenge is transformation. By committing to the daily tasks, exercises, and reflections outlined in this book, you will experience a profound shift in your sales capabilities. This transformation will not only improve your ability to close deals but will also enhance your overall approach to customer interactions, relationship building, and long-term career success.

The 31-day timeframe is intentional. In one month, you can develop habits that will stick, learn to approach challenges with a fresh perspective, and adopt new strategies that will distinguish you from your peers. This is a high-impact, results-driven program that requires dedication, consistency, and a willingness to embrace change.

What to Expect

The 31-Day Car Sales Challenge is structured to guide you through a progressive journey, where each day builds upon the last. This approach ensures that the skills and knowledge you acquire are reinforced and integrated into your daily sales practices.

Day-by-Day Structure

Each day of the challenge focuses on a specific aspect of car sales, from mastering the basics to implementing advanced techniques. The book is divided into four main sections, corresponding to different phases of your journey:

1. **Laying the Foundation (Days 1-7):** The first week is all about setting the stage for your transformation. You will begin by cultivating a strong mindset, understanding your product inside out, and learning to connect

with different types of buyers. This phase establishes the essential building blocks upon which your future success will be built.

2. **Sharpening Your Skills (Days 8-14):** In the second week, you will delve into more specific sales skills. This includes mastering the test drive, refining your negotiation techniques, and learning how to manage your time effectively. By the end of this week, you will have a solid grasp of the key skills that distinguish top performers in car sales.

3. **Advanced Techniques (Days 15-21):** The third week is dedicated to elevating your sales strategy to the next level. You will explore the psychology of selling, learn how to handle difficult customers, and harness the power of storytelling to create compelling sales presentations. This phase is designed to challenge you and push you beyond your comfort zone.

4. **Mastery and Beyond (Days 22-31):** The final week focuses on consolidating your skills and preparing you for long-term success. You will learn how to build lasting relationships with customers, adapt to market changes, and lead others within your sales team. This phase will also encourage you to reflect on your journey and set new goals for the future.

Daily Challenges

Every day presents a specific challenge designed to reinforce the lessons and techniques covered in that day's content. These challenges are practical, actionable tasks that you can immediately apply to your sales activities. They are not meant to be easy—they are designed to push you, stretch your abilities, and help you grow as a sales professional.

For example, on Day 1, you might be tasked with setting a clear sales goal for the day and developing a strategy to achieve it. On Day 5, your challenge could be to practice active listening during customer interactions, noting how this improves the quality of your conversations. These challenges are the heart of the 31-day program, providing you with the hands-on experience needed to internalize new skills.

The Journey Towards Mastery

Mastery in sales is not about memorizing scripts or following a rigid formula. It's about understanding the nuances of human behavior, adapting to the unique needs of each customer, and continuously improving your approach. Throughout this 31-day challenge, you will be encouraged to think critically, reflect on your experiences, and make adjustments where necessary.

This journey is also about self-discovery. As you progress through the book, you will learn more about your strengths, weaknesses, and potential as a sales professional. The daily reflections and exercises are designed to help you gain deeper insights into your personal sales style and how you can leverage it for greater success.

The road ahead may be challenging, but it is also incredibly rewarding. By the end of these 31 days, you will have transformed not only your sales skills but also your mindset and approach to your career. You will emerge from this journey with a renewed sense of confidence, purpose, and a toolkit full of strategies that will serve you for years to come.

Commitment to Success

This book demands your full commitment. The results you achieve will be directly proportional to the effort you put in. By dedicating time each day to complete the exercises, reflect on your progress, and embrace the daily challenges, you will set yourself on the path to becoming a top performer in the car sales industry.

So, as you embark on this journey, remember that transformation doesn't happen overnight. It requires patience, perseverance, and a willingness to step outside of your comfort zone. But with each passing day, you will move closer to your goal of becoming a more effective, confident, and successful sales professional.

Welcome to **The 31-Day Car Sales Challenge**. The road ahead is full of opportunities. All you need to do is take the first step.

Part 1: Laying the Foundation

The first week of The 31-Day Car Sales Challenge is designed to establish a solid foundation for your transformation. These initial days focus on the core principles that will guide you throughout the program. Each day introduces essential concepts and practical exercises, building your confidence and setting you on the path to success.The 31-Day Car Sales Challenge* is designed to establish a solid foundation for your transformation. These initial days focus on the core principles that will guide you throughout the program. Each day introduces essential concepts and practical exercises, building your confidence and setting you on the path to success.

Day 1: Mindset Matters

The journey to becoming a top-performing car salesperson begins with the right mindset. Your mindset influences every aspect of your sales approach, from how you interact with customers to how you handle rejection. A positive, growth-oriented mindset is crucial for overcoming challenges and staying motivated.

Understanding the Importance of a Positive Mindset in Sales

A positive mindset in sales is not just about being optimistic; it's about having the resilience to persist in the face of adversity. In the highly competitive world of car sales, rejection and setbacks are inevitable. How you respond to these challenges will determine your long-term success.

A positive mindset enables you to view setbacks as learning opportunities rather than failures. It empowers you to stay focused on your goals and maintain a high level of energy and enthusiasm, even on difficult days. Moreover, customers are more likely to be drawn to a salesperson who exudes confidence and positivity, as these qualities foster trust and rapport.

Exercises to Develop a Growth-Oriented Mindset

1. **Daily Affirmations**: Start each day with affirmations that reinforce your commitment to growth and success. Phrases like "I am confident in my abilities" or "Every challenge is an opportunity to improve" can help set a positive tone for the day.

2. **Visualization**: Spend a few minutes each day visualizing your success. Picture yourself closing deals, building strong relationships with customers, and achieving your sales goals. Visualization helps condition your mind for success and boosts your confidence.

3. **Gratitude Journaling:** At the end of each day, write down three things you're grateful for, whether they're related to your personal life or your sales career. This practice shifts your focus to the positive aspects of your life and reinforces a growth-oriented mindset.

4. **Mindset Reflection:** Take time to reflect on how your mindset affects your interactions with customers and your overall performance. Identify any negative thought patterns and consciously replace them with positive, growth-focused thoughts.

Day 2: Know Your Product Inside Out

Product knowledge is the backbone of any successful sales strategy. As a car salesperson, you must be intimately familiar with the vehicles you sell. This knowledge enables you to answer customer questions confidently, highlight the benefits of your products, and build credibility with buyers.

Deep Dive into Car Features, Specs, and Benefits

To effectively sell cars, you need to understand more than just the basic features of each model. You should be able to explain the technical specifications, performance capabilities, safety features, and unique selling points of each vehicle in your inventory. This deep knowledge allows you to tailor your sales pitch to the specific needs and preferences of each customer.

For example, if a customer is concerned about fuel efficiency, you should be able to explain the car's engine technology, fuel-saving features, and how it compares to other models in its class. If another customer is interested in safety, you should be prepared to discuss the vehicle's safety ratings, advanced driver-assistance systems, and crash-test results.

Techniques to Communicate Product Knowledge Confidently

1. **Practice Product Demonstrations**: Regularly practice giving product demonstrations to colleagues or in front of a mirror. Focus on clearly explaining the key features and benefits of each car model, and work on delivering this information with confidence and enthusiasm.

2. **Customer-Centric Communication**: When discussing product features, always relate them back to the customer's needs and preferences. For example, instead of just stating that a car has a spacious trunk, explain how this feature would be beneficial for a customer who frequently travels with large luggage or sports equipment.

3. **Stay Updated:** The automotive industry is constantly evolving, with new models, technologies, and trends emerging regularly. Make it a habit to stay informed about the latest developments in the industry, whether through manufacturer training, industry publications, or online

resources.

4. **Overcome Knowledge Gaps**: If a customer asks a question you don't know the answer to, don't be afraid to admit it. However, immediately offer to find the information and follow up with the customer as soon as possible. This approach shows honesty and a commitment to customer satisfaction.

Day 3: Understanding the Buyer

One of the most critical aspects of successful car sales is understanding your buyers. Every customer who walks into your dealership has unique needs, motivations, and concerns. By identifying these factors, you can tailor your approach to meet their expectations and build strong relationships.

Identifying Different Buyer Personas and Their Motivations

Buyers can be broadly categorized into different personas based on their behaviors, preferences, and purchasing motivations. Understanding these personas will help you connect with customers on a deeper level and guide them through the sales process more effectively.

1. **The Practical Buyer:** This persona is focused on value, reliability, and functionality. Practical buyers are often concerned with the car's cost of ownership, fuel efficiency, and maintenance. They may take longer to make a decision and appreciate detailed information and comparisons.

2. **The Status-Seeker**: Status-seekers are drawn to luxury brands, high-end features, and the prestige associated with owning a particular vehicle. They are likely to be interested in the latest technology, design, and brand reputation. Highlighting premium features and exclusivity can resonate with this persona.

3. **The Family-Oriented Buyer**: Family buyers prioritize safety, space, and comfort. They are typically concerned with features like child safety locks, seating capacity, and cargo space. Emphasizing the vehicle's family-friendly attributes will appeal to this group.

4. **The Environmentally Conscious Buyer**: This persona is focused on eco-friendliness and sustainability. They are likely to be interested in hybrid or electric vehicles and appreciate features that reduce the car's

environmental impact. Discussing the vehicle's green credentials and environmental benefits will be important for this buyer.

Building Rapport and Trust with Customers

Trust is the foundation of any successful sales relationship. When customers trust you, they are more likely to share their true concerns and needs, which allows you to provide tailored solutions.

1. **Active Listening**: Truly listen to what the customer is saying, rather than just waiting for your turn to speak. This demonstrates that you value their input and are genuinely interested in meeting their needs.

2. **Empathy**: Show empathy by acknowledging the customer's concerns and expressing understanding. For example, if a customer is worried about financing, reassure them that it's a common concern and that you're here to help them find a solution that works for them.

3. **Consistency**: Be consistent in your interactions with customers. Follow through on promises, such as providing additional information or scheduling a follow-up call. Consistency builds reliability and reinforces trust.

4. **Personal Connection**: Find common ground with your customers, whether it's a shared interest, a similar life experience, or a mutual acquaintance. Personal connections can help break down barriers and create a more relaxed, trusting atmosphere.

Day 4: Setting Daily Goals

In sales, goal-setting is a powerful tool that drives performance and keeps you focused. By setting clear, actionable daily goals, you can measure your progress, stay motivated, and ensure that each day brings you closer to your overall sales objectives.

Importance of Goal-Setting in Sales

Setting goals provides direction and purpose to your daily activities. It helps you prioritize tasks, manage your time effectively, and maintain a high level of productivity. Goals also serve as a benchmark for success, allowing you to track your achievements and identify areas for improvement.

Goals in sales should be specific, measurable, attainable, relevant, and time-bound (SMART). For example, rather than setting a vague goal like "improve my sales," a SMART goal would be "make 10 new customer contacts today and schedule at least 3 test drives."

Creating Actionable, Measurable Daily Goals

1. **Identify Key Activities**: Break down your sales process into key activities, such as prospecting, follow-ups, presentations, and closing. Set daily goals for each of these activities, ensuring that they align with your overall sales targets.

2. **Prioritize High-Impact Tasks**: Focus on tasks that directly contribute

to closing deals and generating revenue. For example, prioritize customer follow-ups over administrative tasks, as the former has a more immediate impact on your sales outcomes.

3. **Track Your Progress**: Use a journal, planner, or digital tool to track your daily goals and monitor your progress. This practice will help you stay accountable and provide valuable insights into your productivity.

4. **Adjust as Needed**: Be flexible and willing to adjust your goals based on your performance and changing circumstances. If a particular strategy isn't yielding results, reassess and set new goals that reflect a different approach.

Day 5: Effective Communication

Effective communication is the cornerstone of successful sales. It involves more than just talking; it requires active listening, clear articulation, and the ability to convey information in a way that resonates with your customers.

Developing Active Listening Skills

Active listening is the ability to fully engage with what the customer is saying, rather than just passively hearing their words. It involves paying attention to both verbal and non-verbal cues, asking clarifying questions, and providing feedback that shows you understand their concerns.

1. **Focus on the Speaker:** When a customer is speaking, give them your full attention. Avoid distractions, maintain eye contact, and refrain from interrupting.

2. **Paraphrase and Reflect**: After the customer has spoken, paraphrase what they've said to ensure you've understood correctly. For example, "So what I'm hearing is that fuel efficiency is a top priority for you. Is that right?" This technique not only confirms your understanding but also shows the customer that you're truly listening.

3. **Ask Open-Ended Questions**: Encourage customers to share more by asking open-ended questions. For example, "What features are most important to you in a new car?" Open-ended questions provide deeper insights into the customer's needs and preferences.

4. **Respond Appropriately**: Your responses should demonstrate empathy and understanding. If a customer expresses concern about a particular feature, acknowledge it and offer a solution or reassurance. For example, "I understand that safety is a major concern for you. This model has received top safety ratings and comes with advanced driver assistance systems."

Crafting Persuasive Pitches That Resonate with Buyers

A persuasive pitch is one that aligns with the customer's needs and addresses their pain points. It's not about hard selling; it's about connecting the dots between what the customer values and what your product offers.

1. **Tailor Your Message**: Customize your pitch to fit the buyer persona you're dealing with. For a practical buyer, focus on the car's reliability and value for money. For a status-seeker, highlight the luxury features and brand prestige. This personalized approach increases the likelihood that your message will resonate with the customer.

2. **Focus on Benefits, Not Just Features**: While it's important to know the features of the car, customers are more interested in how those features will benefit them. For example, instead of just stating that a car has a high fuel efficiency, explain how this translates into significant savings on fuel costs over time.

3. **Use Storytelling**: Incorporate stories into your pitch to make it more engaging and relatable. For example, share a success story of a previous customer who was extremely satisfied with the vehicle. Stories help customers visualize themselves using the product and experiencing the benefits.

4. **Close with a Call to Action:** Every persuasive pitch should end with a clear call to action. This could be an invitation to schedule a test drive, an offer to provide more information, or a prompt to make a purchase decision. Make sure your call to action is specific and easy for the customer to follow.

PART 1: LAYING THE FOUNDATION

Day 6: Overcoming Objections

No matter how well-prepared you are, objections are an inevitable part of the sales process. The key to successful selling is not avoiding objections, but effectively handling them in a way that turns them into opportunities.

Techniques for Handling Common Objections

1. **Listen and Validate**: The first step in overcoming an objection is to listen carefully to the customer's concern. Don't interrupt or dismiss their objection; instead, acknowledge it. For example, if a customer says the price is too high, respond with, "I understand that staying within your budget is important."

2. **Probe for Underlying Concerns:** Sometimes, the initial objection may be masking a deeper concern. Ask probing questions to uncover the real issue. For example, "Is it just the price that's a concern, or are there other factors as well?" Understanding the root of the objection allows you to address it more effectively.

3. **Reframe the Objection**: Turn the objection into a positive by reframing it. For example, if a customer says, "This car is too expensive," you could respond with, "It may seem like a significant investment, but when you consider the long-term savings on fuel and maintenance, it actually offers great value."

4. **Provide Solutions**: Once you've identified the underlying concern,

offer a solution that addresses it. For example, if a customer is worried about financing, discuss flexible payment plans or potential trade-in options. Showing that you're willing to work with them to find a solution can help ease their concerns.

5. **Use the Feel-Felt-Found Method**: This classic sales technique involves empathizing with the customer's objection, relating it to a similar situation, and then providing a positive outcome. For example, "I understand how you feel about the price. Many of my customers have felt the same way, but they found that the car's features and reliability made it well worth the investment."

Turning Objections into Opportunities

1. **View Objections as a Sign of Interest**: An objection often indicates that the customer is seriously considering the purchase but has some reservations. Rather than seeing objections as obstacles, view them as opportunities to further engage with the customer and address their concerns.

2. **Build Trust Through Transparency**: Be honest and transparent when addressing objections. If the customer is concerned about a particular aspect of the car that you know isn't its strongest feature, acknowledge it and provide context. For example, "Yes, this model doesn't have the highest horsepower in its class, but it makes up for it with superior fuel efficiency and safety features."

3. **Follow Up on Objections:** After addressing an objection, follow up to ensure the customer's concerns have been fully resolved. This could

be as simple as asking, "Does that answer your question?" or "Is there anything else you're concerned about?" This shows that you're attentive and committed to finding a solution that works for them.

4. **Leverage Objections in Your Pitch**: Use common objections as part of your pitch to preemptively address concerns. For example, if you know that price is often a sticking point, highlight the car's value and the benefits of investing in it early in your pitch. By addressing potential objections before they arise, you can build confidence and reduce hesitation.

By the end of the first week, you'll have laid a strong foundation for your sales transformation. You'll have developed a positive mindset, gained deep product knowledge, understood your buyers, set daily goals, honed your communication skills, and learned how to effectively handle objections. With these tools at your disposal, you'll be well-prepared to tackle the more advanced challenges in the weeks ahead. Each day builds upon the last, ensuring that your growth is both consistent and cumulative, setting the stage for you to excel in the following phases of **The 30-Day Car Sales Challenge.**

Day 7: Mastering Time Management

Effective time management is crucial in sales, where your ability to prioritize tasks can significantly impact your success.

Prioritizing Tasks and Managing Your Time Effectively

1. **Use a Daily Planner or Digital Calendar**: Start each day by planning your tasks. Use a daily planner or digital calendar to organize your schedule, blocking out time for prospecting, follow-ups, meetings, and other essential tasks. A well-structured schedule helps ensure that you make the most of your time.

2. **Prioritize High-Impact Activities**: Not all tasks are created equal. Focus on high-impact activities that directly contribute to closing sales, such as meeting with clients, giving presentations, and following up with leads. Prioritize these tasks and tackle them during your most productive hours.

3. **Avoid Multitasking:** While it might seem efficient, multitasking can actually reduce your productivity and lead to mistakes. Focus on one task at a time, giving it your full attention before moving on to the next. This approach will improve the quality of your w.ork and help you complete tasks more quickly.

4. **Set Clear Goals for Each Day**: At the start of each day, set clear, achievable goals for what you want to accomplish. These goals could be as simple as making a certain number of follow-up calls, scheduling a

test drive, or closing a deal. Having specific goals keeps you focused and motivated throughout the day.

Reducing Stress and Avoiding Burnout

1. **Take Regular Breaks**: It's important to take regular breaks to avoid burnout and maintain your productivity. Step away from your desk, go for a walk, or take a few minutes to relax. Short breaks can help clear your mind and reduce stress, making you more effective when you return to work.

2. **Delegate When Possible**: If you're overwhelmed with tasks, consider delegating some of them to colleagues or assistants. Delegating allows you to focus on the most critical aspects of your job while ensuring that other tasks are still completed.

3. **Practice Mindfulness and Relaxation Techniques:** Incorporating mindfulness practices, such as deep breathing or meditation, into your daily routine can help reduce stress and improve focus. These techniques are particularly helpful in high-pressure situations, such as negotiations or presentations.

4. **Maintain a Healthy Work-Life Balance**: While dedication is important, it's equally crucial to maintain a healthy work-life balance. Make time for hobbies, family, and relaxation outside of work. A balanced lifestyle will help you stay energized and motivated in your sales career.

By the end of Day 7, you should have a set of time management strategies that will help you stay organized, reduce stress, and avoid burnout.

Effective time management is a key factor in achieving long-term success in sales.

Part 2: Sharpening Your Skills

In the second week of **The 31-Day Car Sales Challenge**, the focus shifts from foundational skills to sharpening the key techniques that differentiate good salespeople from great ones. This part of the book is designed to refine your approach, equipping you with advanced strategies and tools that will help you close more deals, build lasting relationships, and elevate your overall sales performance.

Day 8: Mastering the Test Drive

The test drive is one of the most crucial stages in the car sales process. It's your opportunity to let the car speak for itself while you guide the customer's experience. A well-executed test drive can turn a hesitant prospect into an eager buyer.

Best Practices for Conducting Impactful Test Drives

1. **Preparation is Key**: Before the test drive, make sure the car is clean, well-maintained, and ready to impress. Familiarize yourself with the vehicle's features, and have a route planned that showcases the car's strengths, such as acceleration, handling, and comfort.

2. **Set the Stage**: Begin the test drive by setting expectations. Brief the customer on the route, explain key features they should pay attention to, and encourage them to ask questions throughout. This sets a professional tone and ensures the customer feels informed and comfortable.

3. **Let the Customer Lead**: Give the customer control of the experience. While it's important to highlight features, avoid overwhelming them with too much information at once. Instead, ask questions like, "How does the car feel to drive?" or "What do you think of the ride quality?" This engages the customer and helps you gauge their interest.

4. **Highlight the Vehicle's Unique Selling Points:** During the drive, subtly point out the car's unique features that align with the customer's needs. For instance, if the customer has mentioned safety concerns, highlight the car's advanced safety systems. If they're focused on performance, draw attention to the engine's power and responsiveness.

5. **Create a Memorable Experience**: The goal is to make the test drive memorable. This could be by emphasizing how the car meets the customer's specific needs, or by creating an emotional connection. For example, if the customer mentions they have children, point out the spacious backseat and how it's perfect for family trips.

PART 2: SHARPENING YOUR SKILLS

Creating Memorable Experiences That Lead to Sales

1. **Personalization**: Tailor the test drive to the customer's lifestyle. If they commute long distances, emphasize the car's fuel efficiency and comfort. If they enjoy outdoor activities, highlight the vehicle's cargo space and off-road capabilities. Personalization makes the customer feel understood and valued.

2. **Elicit Emotional Responses**: Buying a car is often an emotional decision. Encourage the customer to imagine themselves owning the car by asking questions like, "Can you see yourself driving this to work every day?" or "How do you think your family would feel about this car?" Eliciting an emotional response can help the customer visualize ownership, making them more likely to buy.

3. **Handle Objections Smoothly**: If the customer expresses concerns during the test drive, address them calmly and confidently. For example, if they mention the car feels too small, acknowledge their concern and suggest alternatives, such as a different model or a package with added features.

4. **Close with Confidence**: After the test drive, gauge the customer's interest by asking for feedback. If they seem enthusiastic, transition into closing the sale by discussing financing options or scheduling a follow-up appointment. The test drive should leave the customer feeling positive and excited about the prospect of owning the car.

Day 9: The Art of Negotiation

Negotiation is where the deal is won or lost. Mastering the art of negotiation requires a delicate balance between achieving your sales goals and ensuring the customer feels they're getting a fair deal. The key is to approach each negotiation with confidence, preparation, and a focus on creating a win-win outcome.

Strategies for Successful Negotiation

1. **Do Your Homework:** Before entering negotiations, know your bottom line and the wiggle room available. Familiarize yourself with the dealership's pricing policies, any current promotions, and the customer's potential budget based on previous conversations.

2. **Build Rapport First**: Establish a connection with the customer before discussing price. Building rapport creates trust, making the customer more likely to be open to your suggestions. Use small talk or shared interests to break the ice and make the negotiation feel less transactional.

3. **Start High, But Fair**: Begin the negotiation with a price that allows room for concessions while still being realistic. This gives you leverage to offer discounts or extras later without sacrificing your profit margin.

4. **Listen More Than You Speak**: Allow the customer to express their concerns or desires fully. Listening carefully gives you valuable insights into what they value most, whether it's price, trade-in value, or additional features. This information is crucial in crafting a deal that

satisfies both parties.

5. **Use Silence to Your Advantage**: After making an offer, remain silent. This puts the ball in the customer's court and can prompt them to reveal more about their willingness to negotiate. Silence can be a powerful tool to encourage the customer to agree to terms closer to your initial offer.

Maintaining Balance Between Customer Satisfaction and Profit

1. **Offer Value, Not Just Discounts**: Instead of immediately dropping the price, offer added value through extras like extended warranties, service packages, or accessories. This approach can satisfy the customer's desire for a deal while maintaining your profit margin.

2. **Know When to Compromise**: Be prepared to make concessions, but know your limits. If a customer is adamant about a lower price, consider offering it in exchange for a quicker sale or a higher down payment. The key is to find compromises that benefit both parties.

3. **Stay Positive and Professional**: Even if negotiations become tense, maintain a positive and professional demeanor. Avoid showing frustration or pressure, as this can erode trust and make the customer feel uncomfortable. A calm, confident approach reassures the customer that they're in good hands.

4. **Close with Confidence:** Once an agreement is reached, reiterate the benefits of the deal to reinforce the customer's decision. Summarize the key points of the agreement and emphasize how it meets the customer's

needs. This final reassurance helps solidify the sale.

Day 10: Building a Referral Network

Referrals are one of the most powerful tools in a salesperson's arsenal. A strong referral network can lead to a steady stream of new customers who come with built-in trust, thanks to the recommendations of satisfied clients. Building and maintaining a referral network requires diligence, excellent customer service, and consistent follow-up.

How to Generate and Maintain a Strong Referral Network

1. **Deliver Exceptional Service**: The foundation of any referral network is outstanding customer service. Ensure every customer interaction is positive, and go above and beyond to meet their needs. Happy customers are more likely to recommend you to their friends and family.

2. **Ask for Referrals:** Don't be shy about asking satisfied customers for referrals. Timing is key—ask for referrals shortly after a successful sale when the customer is still excited about their purchase. For example, you might say, "I'm glad you're happy with your new car. If you know anyone else who's looking, I'd be thrilled to help them too."

3. **Make It Easy for Customers to Refer You:** Provide your customers with business cards, referral forms, or digital links they can easily share

with others. The easier you make it for them to refer you, the more likely they are to do it.

4. **Stay in Touch**: Regular follow-up with past customers helps keep you top of mind for future referrals. Send periodic emails, holiday cards, or service reminders to maintain the relationship. A simple check-in can remind them of the great service you provided and prompt them to refer you to someone they know.

Leveraging Customer Satisfaction for Repeat Business

1. **Create a Referral Incentive Program**: Offer rewards for customers who refer new clients, such as discounts on future services, gift cards, or even cash bonuses. An incentive program not only encourages referrals but also shows customers that you value their recommendations.

2. **Acknowledge and Thank Referrals**: When a customer refers someone to you, acknowledge it promptly and show your appreciation. A personalized thank-you note or a small gift can go a long way in making the customer feel valued and encouraging further referrals.

3. **Follow Up with Referred Customers**: When you receive a referral, contact the referred customer promptly and provide the same high level of service that earned you the referral in the first place. Let them know they were referred by a satisfied customer, which can help build trust from the outset.

4. **Leverage Testimonials**: Use testimonials from satisfied customers as a tool to generate more referrals. Display testimonials on your website,

in marketing materials, or on social media. Potential customers are more likely to trust the experiences of others, making testimonials a powerful referral tool.

Day 11: Time Management for Sales Success

In sales, time is one of your most valuable assets. Effective time management can be the difference between meeting your sales goals and falling short. This day focuses on prioritizing tasks that directly impact sales and creating a daily schedule that maximizes your productivity.

Prioritizing Tasks That Drive Sales

1. **Identify High-Impact Activities**: Determine which activities directly contribute to closing deals, such as prospecting, following up with leads, and conducting test drives. Prioritize these activities over less critical tasks like administrative work or attending meetings that don't lead to immediate sales outcomes. By focusing on high-impact activities, you ensure that your time is spent on actions that move you closer to your goals.

2. **Use the 80/20 Rule**: The Pareto Principle, or 80/20 rule, suggests that 80% of your results come from 20% of your efforts. Identify the top 20% of your activities that generate the most sales and focus your energy on these. This could mean spending more time on follow-up calls with

warm leads rather than cold calling, or prioritizing appointments with high-value clients.

3. **Delegate or Automate Low-Impact Tasks:** Tasks that don't directly contribute to sales should either be delegated or automated. For example, administrative tasks like data entry can be outsourced or handled by software tools, freeing up your time to focus on selling. Utilize customer relationship management (CRM) systems to automate follow-ups, schedule appointments, and manage your leads.

Creating a Daily Schedule That Maximizes Productivity

1. **Morning Power Hours**: Start your day with a "power hour" focused on high-priority tasks, such as prospecting or setting appointments. Morning is often when you have the most energy and focus, so use this time to tackle your most important tasks. This sets a productive tone for the rest of the day.

2. **Block Time for Sales Activities**: Schedule specific blocks of time throughout your day dedicated to key sales activities like follow-up calls, client meetings, and test drives. By setting aside uninterrupted time for these activities, you reduce distractions and increase your efficiency.

3. **End-of-Day Reflection**: Dedicate the last 15 minutes of your workday to review what you've accomplished and plan for the next day. Reflect on what worked well and what didn't, and adjust your strategy accordingly. This reflection helps you continuously improve and ensures that you start the next day with a clear plan of action.

4. **Avoid Multitasking**: Multitasking can decrease productivity and lead to mistakes. Instead, focus on one task at a time, giving it your full attention. This approach not only improves the quality of your work but also helps you complete tasks more efficiently.

5. **Set Boundaries**: Establish clear boundaries between work and personal time. This helps prevent burnout and ensures that when you're working, you're fully focused on your sales tasks. Let clients know your working hours and stick to them, except in cases of urgent matters.

Day 12: Leveraging Social Media

In today's digital age, social media is a powerful tool for car sales professionals. It allows you to reach a larger audience, build your personal brand, and generate leads from platforms where your potential customers are already spending time. This day will teach you how to effectively leverage social media to boost your sales performance.

Utilizing Platforms Like LinkedIn and Instagram for Lead Generation

1. **LinkedIn for Professional Networking**: LinkedIn is a great platform for connecting with potential buyers and other industry professionals. Optimize your LinkedIn profile by highlighting your expertise in car sales and showcasing customer testimonials. Join relevant groups where you can share insights and engage with potential customers. Regularly post content related to car sales, such as tips for buying a car or updates on new models, to establish yourself as an industry expert.

2. **Instagram for Visual Storytelling**: Instagram is ideal for showcasing the cars you sell through high-quality photos and videos. Use Instagram Stories to give followers a behind-the-scenes look at your dealership, highlight new arrivals, or offer car-buying tips. Engage with your audience by responding to comments, running polls, and hosting Q&A sessions. Hashtags can also increase your visibility to users who are searching for specific car models or related content.

3. **Facebook for Community Building**: Facebook allows you to create

a community around your brand. Use it to share detailed posts about the cars you sell, customer success stories, and promotions. Facebook Groups can also be used to create a space for customers and potential buyers to ask questions and share experiences. Running targeted ads on Facebook can help you reach potential customers based on their location, interests, and behavior.

4. **YouTube for In-Depth Content**: If you're comfortable with video content, YouTube is a powerful platform for creating in-depth car reviews, how-to guides, and virtual test drives. Video content can help you build trust with potential buyers who are researching car options online. Make sure to optimize your videos with relevant keywords to increase visibility.

Building a Personal Brand That Attracts Buyers

1. **Consistent Branding Across Platforms:** Ensure that your branding is consistent across all social media platforms. Use the same profile picture, color scheme, and messaging to create a cohesive brand identity. Consistency helps build recognition and trust with your audience.

2. **Provide Value with Every Post**: Focus on providing value to your audience rather than just promoting your products. Share tips, advice, and insights that can help potential buyers make informed decisions. For example, you might post a video explaining the differences between financing options or a blog post about the benefits of leasing versus buying. Valuable content positions you as a trusted advisor rather than just a salesperson.

3. **Engage Regularly with Your Audience**: Social media is a two-way street. Engage with your audience by responding to comments, messages, and questions. Show appreciation for customer loyalty by highlighting their stories and testimonials. Regular engagement not only builds relationships but also keeps you top of mind when they're ready to buy.

4. **Leverage User-Generated Content**: Encourage your satisfied customers to share their experiences on social media and tag you in their posts. User-generated content, such as photos of them with their new car, serves as social proof and can influence others to buy from you. Reposting these on your own channels can also build credibility and showcase real-life success stories.

Day 13: Perfecting Your Follow-Up

Following up with prospects and customers is critical to maintaining momentum in the sales process. A well-timed and thoughtful follow-up can mean the difference between closing a sale and losing a lead. This day focuses on perfecting your follow-up strategy to ensure no opportunity slips through the cracks.

Importance of Timely and Consistent Follow-Up

1. **Strike While the Iron is Hot**: The best time to follow up is when the customer is still thinking about their recent interaction with you. Ideally, follow up within 24-48 hours after a test drive, consultation, or initial inquiry. Prompt follow-up shows that you're attentive and eager to assist, keeping the prospect engaged in the buying process.

2. **Be Consistent Without Being Pushy**: Develop a follow-up schedule that keeps you on the prospect's radar without overwhelming them. For example, if a customer hasn't responded to your initial follow-up, try again a few days later with a different approach, such as offering additional information or a special promotion. The key is to be persistent yet respectful of the customer's time and decision-making process.

3. **Personalize Your Follow-Up:** Personalization is key to effective follow-up. Reference previous conversations, address specific concerns, and tailor your messaging to the customer's needs and interests. For example, if a customer was interested in a specific car model, provide additional details or offer to arrange another test drive.

Tools and Strategies for Effective Follow-Up Communication

1. **CRM Systems**: Utilize customer relationship management (CRM) systems to keep track of all your leads, interactions, and follow-ups. A CRM system allows you to set reminders, automate follow-up emails, and ensure no lead is forgotten. It also helps you segment your leads

based on their stage in the buying process, so you can tailor your follow-up accordingly.

2. **Email Sequences**: Create automated email sequences that nurture leads over time. For example, after an initial inquiry, you might send a series of emails that provide more information about the car they're interested in, share customer testimonials, and offer incentives. Automated emails save time while keeping your prospects engaged.

3. **Text Messaging**: In today's fast-paced world, many customers prefer quick and direct communication. Text messaging can be an effective follow-up tool, especially for confirming appointments or sending quick updates. Just be sure to obtain the customer's consent before texting and keep your messages professional and concise.

4. **Follow-Up Calls**: Sometimes, a phone call is the best way to reconnect with a prospect. Calls allow for a more personal touch and provide an opportunity to address any questions or concerns the customer may have. Prepare for follow-up calls by reviewing your notes and having relevant information ready.

Day 14: Closing the Deal

The culmination of your hard work throughout the sales process is closing the deal. Closing requires skill, timing, and the ability to recognize when the customer is ready to buy. This day is dedicated to honing your closing techniques to ensure you can seal the deal confidently and effectively.

Recognizing Buying Signals and Knowing When to Close

1. **Identify Verbal Cues:** Listen for verbal cues that indicate the customer is ready to buy, such as questions about financing, warranties, or delivery timelines. Statements like, "I really like this car" or "This is exactly what I'm looking for" are strong indicators that the customer is close to making a decision.

2. **Watch for Non-Verbal Cues:** Non-verbal cues, such as nodding, smiling, or closely examining the car, can also signal that the customer is ready to move forward. Pay attention to their body language and respond accordingly.

3. **Ask Trial Closing Questions**: Use trial closing questions to gauge the customer's readiness to buy. Questions like, "Would you like to move forward with this car?" or "Shall we start discussing payment options?" can help you test the waters and prepare for the final close. If the customer responds positively, you can proceed with finalizing the sale.

4. **Overcome Last-Minute Objections**: Even at the closing stage, customers may have last-minute concerns or objections. Address these calmly and confidently, using the information you've gathered throughout the sales process. For example, if the customer is worried about financing, remind them of the payment options you discussed earlier or offer to explain them in more detail. The key is to reassure the customer and make them feel confident in their decision.

Techniques for Sealing the Deal and Ensuring Customer Satisfaction

1. **Assume the Sale**: Once you recognize the buying signals, proceed as if the sale is already confirmed. This might involve asking for the customer's preferred payment method or beginning the paperwork. Assuming the sale creates a smooth transition from discussion to action and reduces the likelihood of hesitation.

2. **Offer an Incentive**: Sometimes, a small incentive can help nudge the customer toward closing. This could be a limited-time discount, a free accessory, or an extended warranty. Ensure that the incentive aligns with the customer's needs and doesn't undermine your profit margins.

3. **Provide Clear Next Steps**: After the customer agrees to the purchase, clearly outline the next steps. This might include completing paperwork, arranging financing, or scheduling delivery. Providing a clear roadmap helps maintain momentum and reduces the chance of buyer's remorse.

4. **Reaffirm the Decision**: Once the deal is closed, reaffirm the customer's decision by highlighting the benefits of their purchase. This could be a quick review of the car's key features or a reminder of how well it suits their needs. Positive reinforcement helps solidify the customer's satisfaction and encourages them to feel confident in their choice.

5. **Ensure a Smooth Handoff**: Whether the next step involves finalizing financing, preparing the car for delivery, or arranging for pick-up, ensure a smooth transition. Coordinate with other departments as needed to make sure everything goes as planned. A seamless handoff enhances the customer experience and reinforces their trust in you and

your dealership.

6. **Follow Up Post-Sale**: Your relationship with the customer doesn't end when the sale is finalized. A follow-up call or email a few days after the purchase shows that you care about their satisfaction and are available for any additional questions or concerns. This step also opens the door for future sales, referrals, and positive reviews.

Remember, closing is not just about making the sale but also ensuring that the customer feels good about their decision. A satisfied customer is more likely to return for future purchases and recommend you to others, which helps build a strong foundation for long-term success in car sales.

Part 3: Advanced Techniques

Day 15: The Psychology of Selling

Understanding buyer psychology is a powerful tool in sales. It allows you to tailor your approach to the way your customers think and make decisions, significantly improving your ability to close deals.

Understanding Buyer Psychology and Decision-Making Processes

1. **Cognitive Biases in Decision-Making:** Buyers are influenced by various cognitive biases, which can impact their purchasing decisions. For example, the "anchoring effect" can make a buyer perceive a car as a good deal when compared to a higher-priced option. Understanding these biases allows you to present information in a way that favors your sales objectives.

2. **Emotional vs. Rational Buying:** Most buyers make purchasing decisions based on emotions, even though they justify them with logic. Identifying the emotional triggers—such as safety, status, or comfort—that resonate with your buyer is crucial. Once you've connected emotionally, you can reinforce their decision with logical arguments, like fuel efficiency or resale value.

3. **The Decision-Making Journey:** Buyers go through several stages before making a purchase, from recognizing a need to evaluating options and finally deciding. As a salesperson, your role is to guide them through this journey, providing the right information and reassurance at each stage. Understanding where your customer is in this process helps you tailor your approach.

Tailoring Sales Strategies to Different Psychological Triggers

1. **Scarcity and Urgency**: Create a sense of urgency by highlighting limited-time offers or low inventory levels. This triggers the psychological fear of missing out (FOMO), encouraging buyers to act quickly.

2. **Social Proof and Authority**: Use testimonials, reviews, and your own expertise to build credibility. When buyers see that others have had positive experiences, or when they perceive you as an authority, they are more likely to trust you and your recommendations.

3. **Reciprocity Principle**: The principle of reciprocity suggests that when you give something to someone, they feel obliged to return the favor. In sales, this could be as simple as offering valuable advice or a small gift, which can make customers more inclined to buy from you.

4. **Consistency and Commitment**: People like to be consistent with their previous actions and commitments. If you can get a buyer to agree to small commitments early in the process, they are more likely to follow through with a purchase to stay consistent with their initial decisions.

By mastering the psychology of selling, you'll be able to influence your buyers' decisions more effectively and close more deals with confidence.

Day 16: Handling Difficult Customers

Difficult customers are an inevitable part of sales, but how you handle them can significantly impact your success and reputation.

Strategies for Managing Challenging Situations with Grace

1. **Stay Calm and Listen**: The first step in dealing with a difficult customer is to remain calm. Listen to their concerns without interrupting, and show empathy by acknowledging their feelings. This helps de-escalate the situation and shows the customer that you are on their side.

2. **Ask Questions to Understand**: Often, difficult customers have underlying concerns that aren't immediately obvious. Ask open-ended questions to get to the root of the issue. Understanding their true concerns allows you to address them more effectively.

3. **Offer Solutions, Not Excuses:** When responding to a difficult customer, focus on offering solutions rather than making excuses. If a mistake was made, own it and propose how you can make it right. Customers appreciate honesty and a proactive approach to problem-solving.

4. **Know When to Escalate**: Sometimes, despite your best efforts, a situation may require escalation to a manager or a different department. Recognize when it's time to involve someone else and ensure the handoff is smooth, so the customer doesn't feel abandoned.

Turning Negative Experiences into Positive Outcomes

1. **Follow Up After Resolution**: After resolving a difficult situation, follow up with the customer to ensure they are satisfied with the outcome. This gesture shows that you care about their experience and can turn a negative situation into a positive one.

2. **Learn from Every Experience**: Use each difficult interaction as a learning opportunity. Reflect on what went well and what could have been handled better. This continuous improvement approach will help you become more adept at handling challenging customers in the future.

3. **Build Resilience**: Dealing with difficult customers can be draining, but it's important to build resilience. Maintain a positive attitude, and don't take negative interactions personally. Focus on the fact that each challenge is an opportunity to improve your skills.

By mastering the art of handling difficult customers, you can turn potential setbacks into opportunities to build stronger relationships and enhance your sales success.

Day 17: The Power of Storytelling

Storytelling is a powerful tool in sales because it allows you to connect with customers on an emotional level and make your message more memorable.

Using Storytelling to Connect Emotionally with Buyers

1. **Create Relatable Scenarios**: When talking about a car's features, frame them within stories that your customers can relate to. For example, instead of just saying a car is safe, tell a story about a family that avoided an accident thanks to the car's advanced safety features. This makes the benefits more tangible and emotionally resonant.

2. **Highlight the Customer's Journey**: Position your customer as the hero of the story. For example, you could tell a story about how a previous buyer went through a similar decision-making process and found the perfect car. This helps the customer visualize themselves in the same situation, making the decision feel more personal and achievable.

Crafting Stories that Highlight the Value of the Car

1. **Focus on Benefits Over Features**: While features are important, stories should focus on the benefits those features provide. For instance, instead of simply stating that a car has great fuel efficiency, tell a story about how a customer saved money on their daily commute and was able to take a road trip with the savings.

2. **Incorporate Visual and Sensory Details**: The more vivid your story, the more it will resonate with the buyer. Incorporate visual and sensory details that help the customer imagine themselves experiencing the benefits of the car. Describe the feeling of the leather seats, the sound of the engine, or the ease of navigating through traffic. These details make your story more engaging and persuasive.

3. **Use Testimonials as Stories**: Testimonials from satisfied customers are a form of storytelling that adds credibility to your sales pitch. Share stories of how other buyers have benefited from the car you're selling. For example, "John, a client of ours, was initially hesitant about buying a new SUV. But after experiencing the smooth ride and realizing how much it improved his family road trips, he couldn't be happier with his decision."

4. **End with a Strong Call to Action**: A compelling story should conclude with a clear and persuasive call to action. After telling a story about a happy customer, you might say, "Just like John, you too can enjoy these benefits. Let's take the next step and see how this car fits your needs."

Mastering the art of storytelling can help to make your sales presentations more compelling and increase your ability to connect with customers on an emotional level.

Day 18: Creating a Winning Sales Presentation

A well-structured sales presentation is crucial to engaging your audience and persuading them to make a purchase.

Structuring Presentations that Engage and Persuade

1. **Start with a Strong Opening**: Your presentation should begin with a compelling hook that grabs your audience's attention. This could be a surprising fact, a question that resonates with their needs, or a brief, impactful story. The goal is to immediately engage your audience and set the tone for the rest of the presentation.

2. **Clearly Define the Problem:** Before diving into the solution, clearly outline the problem your customer is facing. This helps to align their needs with what you're offering. For example, if you're selling a family car, you might start by discussing the challenges of finding a vehicle that is both safe and spacious.

3. **Present the Solution:** After defining the problem, present the car as the solution. Highlight how it addresses the specific needs and concerns of the buyer. Use a logical flow that builds on the information you've already shared, making it easy for the customer to follow and understand why this car is the best choice for them.

4. **Incorporate Demonstrations and Visuals:** A great presentation isn't just about talking; it's about showing. Incorporate demonstrations, videos, or visuals that reinforce your points. For example, you could

show a short video of the car's safety features in action or a graphic comparing its fuel efficiency to that of competitors.

Using Visuals and Data to Reinforce Key Points

1. **Simplify Complex Information**: Use visuals to break down complex data or technical specifications into digestible chunks. For instance, instead of listing out all the safety features, present them in a clear, visual format, such as an infographic that shows how each feature contributes to overall safety.

2. **Highlight Key Benefits**: Use charts, graphs, or bullet points to emphasize the car's key benefits. Visuals can help reinforce your message and make it more memorable. For example, a bar graph comparing the maintenance costs of your car versus competitors can visually demonstrate long-term savings.

3. **Keep It Clean and Professional**: Ensure your visuals are clean, professional, and not cluttered. Too much information or overly complex visuals can confuse your audience and detract from your message. Stick to high-quality images and clear, concise data presentations.

4. **Practice, Practice, Practice:** The key to a successful presentation is practice. Rehearse your presentation multiple times to ensure smooth delivery. Practice will help you refine your message, improve your timing, and boost your confidence, ensuring that you can deliver a persuasive and impactful presentation.

Towards the end of Day 18, you should be equipped with the skills to create and deliver presentations that not only engage your audience but also persuade them to make a purchase.

Day 19: Personal Development for Sales Success

Personal growth and continuous learning are essential for long-term success in sales. Day 19 focuses on how you can invest in yourself to maintain and improve your sales skills.

Continuous Learning and Self-Improvement Techniques

1. **Embrace Lifelong Learning**: The most successful salespeople are those who continually seek to improve their knowledge and skills. This could involve reading books, attending workshops, or following industry blogs and podcasts. Dedicate time each week to learning something new that can enhance your sales techniques.

2. **Seek Feedback and Reflect**: Regularly seek feedback from colleagues, managers, and even customers. Constructive criticism is invaluable for personal growth. After each sale or interaction, take time to reflect on what went well and what could be improved. This habit of reflection will help you fine-tune your approach over time.

3. **Set Personal Development Goals:** Just as you set sales targets, set personal development goals. These might include improving your negotiation skills, learning a new sales technique, or increasing your product knowledge. Regularly review your progress and adjust your

goals as needed.

Setting Long-Term Career Goals Beyond the 31-Day Challenge

1. **Identify Your Career Aspirations:** Think about where you want to be in the next five to ten years. Do you see yourself in a management role, or perhaps leading a sales team? Identifying your long-term career goals will help you stay motivated and focused on continuous improvement.

2. **Create a Roadmap for Success:** Once you have a clear vision of your long-term goals, create a roadmap to achieve them. This might involve taking on additional responsibilities, pursuing further education, or building a network of mentors and peers who can support your growth.

3. **Stay Committed to Growth**: Personal and professional growth is a journey, not a destination. Stay committed to developing your skills and knowledge, and be open to new opportunities and challenges. A growth mindset will help you stay adaptable and successful in an ever-changing sales environment.

Focusing on personal development not only enhance your sales skills but also set the foundation for a successful and fulfilling career in the automotive industry.

Day 20: Ethical Selling

Ethical selling is about maintaining integrity and transparency in your sales practices, which builds trust and long-term relationships with your customers.

Maintaining Integrity and Transparency in Sales Practices

1. **Be Honest About the Product:** Always be honest about the cars you're selling, including both the positives and potential drawbacks. Misrepresenting a product may lead to a quick sale, but it will harm your reputation and lead to dissatisfied customers. Transparency builds trust, which is essential for repeat business and referrals.

2. **Respect the Customer's Needs**: Ethical selling means prioritizing the customer's needs over making a sale. Listen carefully to what the customer is looking for, and if your product isn't the right fit, be honest about it. Helping customers find the right solution, even if it means losing a sale, builds credibility and trust.

3. **Avoid High-Pressure Tactics**: While it's important to close deals, avoid using high-pressure tactics that make customers feel uncomfortable. Instead, focus on educating the customer and providing them with the information they need to make an informed decision. Ethical selling creates a positive buying experience and fosters long-term customer relationships.

PART 3: ADVANCED TECHNIQUES

Building a Reputation for Honesty and Reliability

1. **Be Consistent in Your Actions**: Building a reputation for honesty requires consistency. Ensure that your words and actions align, and that you deliver on promises. Customers appreciate reliability, and consistent, ethical behavior will earn their trust and loyalty.

2. **Handle Mistakes with Integrity**: If you make a mistake, own up to it and take steps to correct it. Customers understand that mistakes happen, but how you handle them can make or break your reputation. Addressing issues promptly and fairly will enhance your reputation as a trustworthy and ethical salesperson.

3. **Encourage Ethical Practices in Your Team**: If you're in a leadership position, foster a culture of ethical behavior within your team. Lead by example, and encourage others to prioritize honesty and transparency in their sales practices. A team committed to ethical selling will enhance the overall reputation of your dealership.

By the end of Day 20, you should have a strong understanding of the importance of ethical selling and how it contributes to long-term success. Ethical sales practices not only build trust and customer loyalty but also ensure that you can be proud of the work you do.

Day 21: Analyzing Your Sales Performance

Analyzing your sales performance is critical for ongoing improvement and long-term success. Day 21 focuses on how to reflect on your progress, identify areas for improvement, and use data to refine your sales approach.

Reflecting on Progress and Identifying Areas for Improvement

1. **Review Your Sales Metrics**: Start by reviewing your sales metrics over the past 21 days. Look at your conversion rates, average deal size, and the number of follow-ups it took to close deals. These metrics will give you a clear picture of your strengths and areas where you need to improve.

2. **Identify Patterns and Trends:** Look for patterns or trends in your sales performance. For example, do you close more deals at certain times of the day, or with specific types of customers? Understanding these patterns can help you tailor approach to maximize your strengths and address any weaknesses.

3. **Seek Feedback from Peers and Mentors**: Don't rely solely on your own analysis. Seek feedback from colleagues, managers, or mentors who can offer a different perspective on your performance. They might notice things you've overlooked or provide insights on how to improve your sales techniques.

4. **Reflect on Your Customer Interactions**: Think back on your inter-

actions with customers. Were there moments where you could have communicated more effectively, or situations where you might have handled objections better? Reflecting on these interactions will help you refine your approach in future sales.

Using Data to Refine Your Sales Strategy

1. **Analyze Customer Feedback**: If your dealership collects customer feedback, use this data to identify areas for improvement. Pay attention to common themes or complaints, and think about how you can adjust your sales approach to address these issues. Positive feedback can also highlight what you're doing well and should continue to emphasize.

2. **Track Follow-Up Success**: Review the effectiveness of your follow-up strategy. Analyze how many follow-ups it typically takes to close a sale and consider whether certain follow-up methods (e.g., email vs. phone) are more effective than others. Use this data to optimize your follow-up process.

3. **Refine Your Pitch Based on Conversion Rates**: If you notice that certain aspects of your sales pitch consistently lead to higher conversion rates, double down on those elements. Conversely, if parts of your pitch aren't resonating with customers, consider revising them. Data-driven adjustments can significantly improve your overall sales performance.

4. **Set New Goals Based on Your Analysis**: After analyzing your performance, set new goals for the remainder of the 30-day challenge. These goals should be specific, measurable, and based on the areas where you've identified the most potential for improvement. For example, if

you notice that your close rate drops during follow-ups, set a goal to improve your follow-up strategy and increase your close rate by a certain percentage.

By the end of Day 21, you'll have a clearer understanding of your sales performance, as well as actionable steps to enhance your sales strategy. Continuous analysis and refinement are key to maintaining high performance and achieving long-term success in car sales.

Day 22: Advanced Negotiation Techniques

Negotiation is an art that can significantly impact your sales success. Day 22 focuses on advanced negotiation techniques to help you close deals on favorable terms.

PART 3: ADVANCED TECHNIQUES

Mastering the Art of Negotiation

1. **Understand the Customer's Needs and Wants:** Effective negotiation starts with a deep understanding of the customer's needs and wants. Ask open-ended questions and listen carefully to their responses. The more you know about what they're looking for, the better you can tailor your negotiation strategy to meet their expectations.

2. **Build Rapport Before Negotiating**: Building rapport with the customer before entering negotiations can make them more inclined to work with you. Establish a connection by showing genuine interest in their needs, being friendly, and creating a positive, relaxed atmosphere.

3. **Use the "Good Cop, Bad Cop" Technique Carefully**: This technique involves one person being tough on price or terms while the other is more flexible and understanding. If you're working as part of a team, this approach can be effective, but use it carefully to avoid coming across as manipulative.

4. **Know Your Bottom Line**: Before entering negotiations, determine your bottom line—the minimum terms you're willing to accept. Knowing this in advance will help you stay firm and avoid making concessions that could undermine your profitability.

Closing Deals with Confidence

1. **Use Silence to Your Advantage**: Silence can be a powerful tool in negotiations. After making an offer, remain silent and let the customer

speak next. The silence often prompts them to reveal more information or reconsider their position, giving you the upper hand.

2. **Present Multiple Options**: Offering multiple options can make the customer feel more in control and reduce resistance. For example, you could present different financing plans or packages, allowing them to choose the one that best fits their needs. This approach often leads to a quicker and more satisfactory close.

3. **Use Scarcity and Urgency**: Creating a sense of scarcity or urgency can motivate customers to act quickly. For instance, if there's limited availability of a popular model or a special promotion that's ending soon, emphasize this to create urgency. However, it's crucial to be honest and transparent; false urgency can damage trust and harm your reputation.

4. **Be Willing to Walk Away**: One of the most powerful negotiation tactics is the willingness to walk away. If the deal doesn't meet your minimum requirements or the customer is making unreasonable demands, don't be afraid to step back. This approach often makes the customer reconsider their position, and in many cases, they may return with a more reasonable offer.

5. **Close with Confidence**: When you're ready to close the deal, do so with confidence. Clearly outline the final terms and ask for the customer's agreement. Use a positive tone and language that assumes they're ready to move forward, such as "When would you like to schedule the delivery?" or "Let's finalize the paperwork so you can start enjoying your new car."

By the end of Day 22, you'll have honed your negotiation skills, allowing you to close deals on terms that are favorable to both you and your customers. These advanced techniques will help you navigate complex negotiations with ease and confidence.

.

Part 4: Mastery and Beyond

As you approach the final stretch of the 31-day challenge, the focus shifts from foundational skills to advanced strategies that will solidify your place as a top-performing car sales professional. These final days are designed to take you from proficient to masterful, ensuring that you not only excel in your current role but also set the stage for future growth and leadership.

Day 23: Building Long-Term Relationships

Turning One-Time Buyers into Lifelong Customers

The true mark of a successful sales professional isn't just in closing the sale but in ensuring that the customer returns and refers others. Long-term relationships are the bedrock of a sustainable sales career, and this day is dedicated to mastering the art of turning one-time buyers into loyal, repeat customers.

Start by understanding the lifetime value of a customer. When you shift your focus from the immediate sale to the long-term potential, your approach changes. It's no longer just about making the sale today; it's about creating an experience that will make the customer come back tomorrow, next year, and beyond.

To build these relationships, always follow up after the sale, not just for the obligatory check-in but with genuine interest. Personalized communication, remembering details about their preferences, and offering value even after the transaction, like sending them information on a new model they might like, can keep you top of mind.

Strategies for Maintaining Ongoing Communication and Engagement

Engagement doesn't stop at the sale—it's an ongoing process. Use a mix of automated and personal communication methods to stay in touch. For example, schedule regular check-ins using your CRM, send personalized emails on birthdays or purchase anniversaries, and offer exclusive deals to past customers.

Additionally, consider organizing or participating in community events, such as car shows or charity drives, where you can interact with your customers outside the sales environment. This not only strengthens relationships but also positions you as a trusted member of the community.

Day 24: Adapting to Market Changes

Staying Agile and Responsive to Shifts in the Automotive Industry

The automotive industry is constantly evolving, driven by technological advancements, economic factors, and consumer preferences. To remain successful, you must stay agile and responsive to these shifts. This day focuses on developing the foresight and adaptability needed to thrive in a dynamic market.

Start by regularly educating yourself on industry trends. Whether it's attending industry conferences, subscribing to automotive publications, or participating in webinars, staying informed will give you the insight needed to anticipate changes and adapt your strategies accordingly.

Innovating Sales Techniques to Match Market Trends

Innovation is key to staying ahead of the competition. As the market changes, so should your sales techniques. For example, if there's a growing demand for electric vehicles, ensure you're well-versed in their unique selling points and the concerns potential buyers may have.

Experiment with new sales approaches, such as virtual car tours or live Q&A sessions on social media. Test different strategies and continuously refine your approach based on customer feedback and market responses. The ability to pivot quickly will keep you relevant and successful in a fluctuating market.

Day 25: Leadership in Sales

Leading by Example and Mentoring Other Sales Professionals

As you develop mastery in sales, a natural next step is to take on a leadership role. This doesn't necessarily mean becoming a manager; leadership can be demonstrated by mentoring others, sharing your knowledge, and leading by example.

On this day, focus on the qualities that make an effective leader in sales—integrity, empathy, and a commitment to excellence. Be the person others look up to for guidance and inspiration. Whether it's offering advice to a struggling colleague or sharing best practices in team meetings, your contributions will help elevate the entire team.

Building a Culture of Success Within Your Sales Team

Creating a culture of success involves more than just personal achievement; it's about fostering an environment where everyone can thrive. Encourage collaboration rather than competition, celebrate team successes, and promote continuous learning and development.

As you lead by example, your positive attitude and strong work ethic will set the tone for others. A successful team is built on trust, respect, and shared goals—be the catalyst that drives this culture forward.

Day 26: Leveraging Technology

Using CRM Tools, AI, and Other Technologies to Enhance Sales

Technology has revolutionized the way sales are conducted, offering tools that can significantly enhance your efficiency and effectiveness. Today's focus is on leveraging these technologies to optimize your sales process and build stronger customer relationships.

Start by mastering your CRM system. Use it not just as a database but as a tool for automating follow-ups, tracking customer interactions, and analyzing sales performance. CRM tools can help you manage leads more effectively, ensuring that no potential sale slips through the cracks.

Artificial Intelligence (AI) is another powerful tool in modern sales. AI can help you predict customer behavior, personalize communication, and even suggest the best times to reach out to prospects. Familiarize yourself with the AI tools available in your industry and integrate them into your sales strategy.

Automating Tasks to Focus on Building Relationships

Automation can free up time for what really matters—building relationships. Use automation for routine tasks like sending follow-up emails or scheduling appointments, so you can focus on the human aspects of sales that technology can't replicate. By automating these processes, you can ensure consistency while dedicating more time to understanding your customers' needs and building trust.

Day 27: The Importance of Networking

Building a Strong Professional Network for Long-Term Success

Networking is a critical component of a successful sales career. A strong professional network can provide new leads, referrals, and opportunities for collaboration. On this day, focus on strategies for building and maintaining a robust network that will support your long-term success.

Attend industry events, join professional associations, and participate in online forums where you can connect with peers and potential clients. Networking isn't just about exchanging business cards—it's about building genuine relationships that can benefit all parties involved.

Attending Events and Joining Communities that Boost Visibility

Visibility is key to building your personal brand and establishing yourself as a leader in the industry. Attend events, both virtual and in-person, where you can showcase your expertise, share insights, and learn from others. Consider speaking at conferences or writing articles for industry publications to increase your visibility further.

Joining communities, whether they're local business groups or online sales forums, allows you to connect with like-minded professionals and stay engaged with the latest industry developments. These connections can lead to valuable partnerships, new opportunities, and a steady stream of referrals.

Day 28: Financial Literacy for Sales Professionals

Understanding Commission Structures and Managing Income

Financial literacy is essential for long-term career success. Understanding how commission structures work, managing your income, and planning for financial stability are crucial skills for any sales professional. This day is dedicated to developing a strong foundation in financial management.

Start by thoroughly understanding your commission structure. Know how you're paid, what incentives are available, and how you can maximize your earnings. Additionally, learn to manage your income effectively—set aside funds for taxes, save for slow months, and invest in your professional development.

Making Smart Financial Decisions to Support a Stable Career

Smart financial decisions extend beyond managing your current income—they involve planning for the future. Consider working with a financial advisor to develop a plan for saving, investing, and growing your wealth over time. This planning will provide financial stability and allow you to focus on your career without the stress of financial uncertainty.

Being financially literate also means understanding the financial aspects of your sales role, such as how discounts and financing options impact your commissions and how to structure deals that benefit both you and your customers.

Day 29: Developing a Personal Sales Brand

Creating a Distinct Personal Brand that Stands Out in the Market

Your personal brand is what sets you apart from other sales professionals. It's how you present yourself to clients, colleagues, and the broader market. On this day, focus on developing a distinct personal brand that reflects your values, strengths, and unique selling points.

Start by defining what you want to be known for in the industry. Are you the go-to expert for a specific type of vehicle? Do you have a reputation for exceptional customer service? Whatever it is, make sure it's consistent in all your interactions, from how you communicate with clients to how you present yourself online.

Consistency in Messaging and Customer Interactions

Consistency is key to building a strong personal brand. Ensure that your messaging is uniform across all platforms—whether it's your social media profiles, email communications, or face-to-face interactions. This consistency builds trust and reinforces your brand identity.

Develop a personal marketing plan that includes regular social media posts, blog articles, and networking activities that showcase your expertise. Over time, these efforts will establish you as a leader in your field and attract new clients who resonate with your brand.

PART 4: MASTERY AND BEYOND

Day 30: Scaling Your Sales Efforts

Expanding Your Reach Through Partnerships and New Channels

Scaling your sales efforts means looking beyond individual sales to opportunities for growth through partnerships, new sales channels, and broader market reach. This day is about thinking strategically about how to expand your influence and increase your sales volume.

Identify potential partnerships with businesses that complement your offerings, such as local car service centers, insurance providers, or aftermarket parts dealers. These partnerships can create referral opportunities and offer added value to your customers.

Explore new sales channels, such as online car sales platforms, and consider how you can leverage these to reach a wider audience. Expanding your sales efforts might also involve venturing into new markets or regions where there is unmet demand for your expertise and services. By broadening your reach, you can tap into new customer segments and increase your overall sales potential.

Identifying Opportunities for Career Growth and Development

Scaling your sales efforts isn't just about making more sales; it's also about advancing your career. Take the time to identify opportunities for growth within your current organization or consider new roles that align with your long-term goals.

For instance, if you've mastered individual sales, you might explore a transition into sales management, where you can lead and mentor a team. Alternatively, you could specialize in a high-demand area, such as luxury vehicles or fleet sales, to position yourself as an expert in that niche.

Continuous learning is crucial to scaling your career. Invest in advanced sales training, attend leadership workshops, or pursue certifications that enhance your skill set. By proactively seeking out opportunities for development, you can ensure that your career trajectory aligns with your aspirations.

Day 31: Celebrating Success and Setting Future Goals

Reflecting on Achievements and Celebrating Milestones

As you reach the final day of the 31-day challenge, it's important to take a step back and reflect on your journey. Celebrate the successes, both big and small, that you've achieved over the past month. Whether it's closing a significant deal, overcoming a challenging situation, or simply growing as a sales professional, these milestones are worth acknowledging.

Celebrating your achievements isn't just about patting yourself on the back—it's about recognizing the hard work, dedication, and persistence that brought you to this point. This reflection helps reinforce positive behaviors and motivates you to continue striving for excellence.

Consider organizing a small celebration or reward for yourself, whether it's treating yourself to something special or sharing your success with colleagues who supported you along the way. Recognizing your progress reinforces the value of your efforts and sets a positive tone for the future.

Setting New Goals for Continuous Improvement Beyond the 31 Days

The end of this challenge is not the end of your journey—it's the beginning of a new chapter in your career. Use this day to set new goals that will continue to push you forward. Reflect on what you've learned, the skills you've developed, and the areas where you can continue to grow.

Set both short-term and long-term goals. Short-term goals might include closing a certain number of deals next month or mastering a specific sales technique. Long-term goals could involve advancing to a leadership position, increasing your income, or expanding your professional network.

Ensure that your goals are SMART (Specific, Measurable, Achievable, Relevant, and Time-bound). This framework will help you stay focused and motivated as you work towards achieving them.

Additionally, consider creating a personal development plan that includes ongoing education, networking, and skill-building activities. This plan will serve as a roadmap for your continued growth and ensure that you remain on track to achieve your long-term aspirations.

Embracing the Journey of Mastery

Mastery in sales is not a destination but a continuous journey. Over these 30 days, you've developed a solid foundation, advanced your skills, and begun to master the art of car sales. But the path to success doesn't end here—it's an ongoing process of learning, adapting, and growing.

By embracing the principles and techniques outlined in this challenge, you've set yourself on a course for long-term success. Remember that every day presents a new opportunity to improve, innovate, and achieve. Keep pushing the boundaries of what's possible, and never stop striving for excellence.

As you move forward, continue to build on the momentum you've created.

PART 4: MASTERY AND BEYOND

Stay committed to your personal and professional development, and always seek out new ways to elevate your sales game. With dedication, perseverance, and a passion for what you do, there's no limit to what you can achieve in the world of car sales.

This 31-day challenge is just the beginning of your journey towards becoming a top performer in your field. Keep the lessons you've learned close, and let them guide you as you navigate the ever-evolving landscape of car sales. Your success story is just beginning—write it with purpose, passion, and the confidence that you are equipped to achieve greatness.

The Journey Continues

Encouraging Readers to Keep Applying the Skills Learned

As you reach the final pages of "**The 31-Day Car Sales Challenge: Transform Your Sales Skills**," it's important to recognize that while the structured challenge may be complete, your journey as a sales professional is far from over. The skills, techniques, and strategies you've acquired over the past 31 days are not just tools to be used once—they are foundational elements of your ongoing success in the car sales industry.

The journey you've embarked upon is one of continuous application and refinement. The market, customer preferences, and sales environments are always evolving, which means that the skills you've learned must be consistently applied, tested, and adapted. This is where true mastery lies—not in the completion of the challenge, but in the commitment to constantly sharpen and utilize your skills in real-world situations.

Remember, every interaction with a customer is an opportunity to apply what you've learned. Whether it's practicing the art of negotiation, using storytelling to connect with a buyer, or leveraging technology to enhance your sales approach, each day presents a chance to put these strategies into action. By doing so, you'll not only reinforce your learning but also see tangible results in your sales performance.

Don't let the completion of this challenge signal the end of your development. Instead, view it as the beginning of a lifelong commitment to excellence in your career. Keep revisiting the lessons from this book whenever you encounter new challenges or need a refresher on key concepts. The knowledge contained within these pages is a resource that can serve you throughout your career, helping you to adapt to new trends, overcome obstacles, and consistently achieve your sales goals.

Motivating the Reader to Pursue Excellence in Their Sales Career

The path to excellence is rarely linear, but it is always rewarding. As a car sales professional, your journey will be filled with highs and lows, victories and setbacks. The key to long-term success lies in your ability to remain resilient, motivated, and focused on continuous improvement.

Excellence in sales is not just about closing deals—it's about becoming a trusted advisor to your customers, someone they can rely on for honest advice, superior service, and a genuine commitment to their satisfaction. It's about building a reputation that sets you apart in the industry, one that is built on integrity, expertise, and unwavering dedication.

To pursue excellence, you must be willing to push beyond your comfort zone, to take risks, and to learn from your experiences—both the successes and the failures. The car sales industry is dynamic, and those who excel are the ones who embrace change, seek out new opportunities for growth, and constantly strive to enhance their skills.

Set ambitious goals for yourself, both in terms of your sales targets and your professional development. Pursue certifications, attend industry seminars, and network with other top performers in your field. By continuously investing in your growth, you'll not only achieve your career aspirations but also set a standard of excellence that others will aspire to follow.

Moreover, excellence in sales is about more than just individual achievement. It's about contributing to the success of your team, mentoring others, and elevating the overall performance of your organization. By sharing the knowledge and skills you've acquired, you can help create a culture of excellence within your workplace, one that encourages everyone to strive for greatness.

As you move forward in your career, keep the lessons of this 31-day challenge at the forefront of your mind. Let them guide your actions, inform your decisions, and inspire you to reach new heights. Remember that every day is an opportunity to become better, to refine your approach, and to deliver even greater value to your customers.

In conclusion, the journey to becoming a master in car sales is ongoing, and it's one that requires dedication, passion, and a relentless pursuit of excellence. By continuing to apply the skills you've learned and maintaining a mindset focused on growth, there's no limit to what you can achieve. Your career is in your hands—shape it with the same determination and enthusiasm that brought you to this point, and success will surely follow. The journey continues, and with it, so does the potential for greatness.

Appendix: Tools and Resources for Sales Professionals

The appendix serves as a valuable resource hub, offering tools, templates, and recommendations that will support your ongoing development as a sales professional. The purpose of this section is to provide you with easy access to materials that can enhance your knowledge, streamline your daily activities, and equip you with practical strategies for continuous improvement in the car sales industry.

List of Recommended Books, Websites, and Tools for Further Learning

Books

1. **"How to Win Friends and Influence People"** by **Dale Carnegie**
   This classic book is essential for anyone in sales. Carnegie's insights into human behavior and communication will help you build stronger relationships with customers, improve your persuasion skills, and ultimately close more sales.

2. **"SPIN Selling"** by **Neil Rackham**

This book introduces the SPIN (Situation, Problem, Implication, Need-Payoff) technique, which is a proven method for handling complex sales. It's particularly valuable for car sales professionals who deal with high-stakes transactions.

3. **"The Challenger Sale"** by **Matthew Dixon and Brent Adamson**

Dixon and Adamson explore the idea that the most successful salespeople are those who challenge their customers' thinking and provide unique insights. This book will help you develop a sales approach that differentiates you from the competition.

4. **"Influence: The Psychology of Persuasion"** by **Robert Cialdini**

Understanding the principles of influence and persuasion is crucial in sales. Cialdini's book provides a deep dive into how these principles work, equipping you with strategies to ethically persuade customers and close deals.

5. **"The Little Red Book of Selling"** by **Jeffrey Gitomer**

Gitomer's book is packed with practical advice and tips for increasing sales. It's a quick read, but one that's filled with actionable insights that you can apply immediately in your day-to-day sales activities.

Websites

1. **HubSpot Sales Blog**

The HubSpot Sales Blog offers a wealth of articles, guides, and tips on all aspects of sales. It's a great resource for staying updated on the latest trends and best practices in the industry.

Website: blog.hubspot.com/sales

2. **Sales Hacker**

Sales Hacker is a leading resource for sales professionals, offering articles, webinars, and podcasts on various sales topics. Whether you're looking for advice on closing techniques, sales technology, or lead generation, Sales Hacker has you covered.

Website: [saleshacker.com](https://www.saleshacker.com/)

3. **Close.com Blog**

Close.com provides actionable sales advice and strategies, particularly for those in the SaaS and tech industries. However, many of the insights are applicable to car sales as well, especially in the areas of customer relationship management and closing strategies.

Website: blog.close.com

4. **LinkedIn Sales Solutions**

LinkedIn is a powerful tool for sales professionals, and their Sales Solutions blog offers tips on how to leverage the platform for lead generation, networking, and personal branding.

Website: business.linkedin.com/sales-solutions

5. **The Sales Blog** by **Anthony Iannarino**

Anthony Iannarino is a well-known sales expert, and his blog offers in-depth articles on various aspects of sales, from mindset and motivation

to practical techniques for improving your performance.
Website: [thesalesblog.com](https://www.thesalesblog.com/)

Tools

1. **Customer Relationship Management (CRM) Software**
   - **Salesforce**: Salesforce is a leading CRM tool that helps you manage customer relationships, track sales leads, and automate many of your sales tasks. It's an essential tool for any sales professional looking to stay organized and maximize productivity.
   - **HubSpot CRM**: HubSpot offers a free CRM that's easy to use and packed with features to help you manage your sales pipeline, track customer interactions, and improve your follow-up process.

2. **Sales Enablement Tools**
   - **Yesware**: Yesware is an email tracking tool that integrates with your email platform to track when recipients open your emails or click on links. It also provides templates and other tools to streamline your email communication.
   - **Seismic**: Seismic is a sales enablement platform that helps you deliver personalized content to your prospects and customers, ensuring that your messaging is always relevant and impactful.

3. **Lead Generation Tools**
   - **LinkedIn Sales Navigator:** LinkedIn's Sales Navigator is a powerful tool for finding and connecting with potential leads. It allows you to filter LinkedIn's vast network to find prospects that match your target criteria.
   - **ZoomInfo**: ZoomInfo provides detailed contact and company information, helping you to identify and reach out to potential leads with

precision.

4. **Productivity Tools**
   - **Trello**: Trello is a project management tool that helps you organize your tasks and keep track of your progress. It's useful for managing your daily sales activities and ensuring that you stay on top of your goals.
   - **Evernote**: Evernote is a note-taking app that allows you to capture ideas, take notes during meetings, and keep track of important information. It's an excellent tool for staying organized and ensuring that you don't miss any important details.

Templates and Worksheets for Daily Sales Activities

Daily Sales Activity Tracker

APPENDIX: TOOLS AND RESOURCES FOR SALES PROFESSIONALS

Use this template to track your daily sales activities, including the number of calls made, emails sent, follow-ups completed, and deals closed. This tracker will help you stay organized and ensure that you are consistently working towards your sales goals.

Goal-Setting Worksheet

GOAL WORKSHEET

DATE:

GOAL:

WHY?

STEPS TO TAKE
-
-
-
-

NOTES

This worksheet is designed to help you set actionable and measurable goals for each day. It includes sections for outlining your goals, identifying the steps needed to achieve them, and tracking your progress. By using this worksheet, you'll be able to stay focused and ensure that your daily activities align with your long-term objectives.

Customer Persona Template

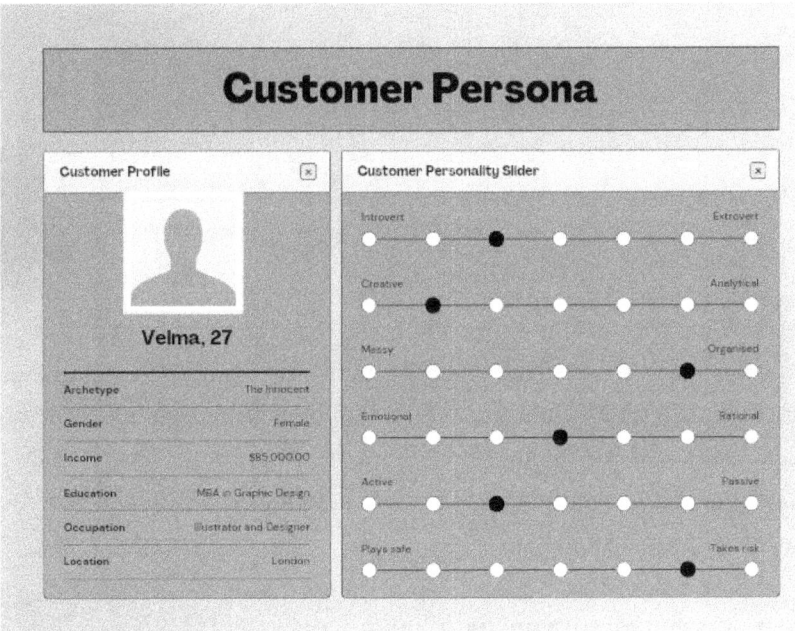

Understanding your customers is key to successful selling. This template allows you to create detailed customer personas, including demographic information, buying motivations, and potential objections. By filling out this template for each of your target customer groups, you'll be better prepared to tailor your sales approach to meet their needs.

Follow-Up Email Templates

Follow-up is critical in sales, and these templates provide you with a starting point for crafting effective follow-up emails. The templates include different scenarios, such as following up after a test drive, checking in after a meeting, or sending a thank-you note after a purchase. Customize these templates to fit your personal style and the specific needs of your customers.

Sales Presentation Template

APPENDIX: TOOLS AND RESOURCES FOR SALES PROFESSIONALS

This template helps you structure your sales presentations, ensuring that you cover all the key points while keeping your audience engaged. It includes sections for introducing the product, highlighting its benefits, addressing potential objections, and closing the sale. Use this template to create consistent and compelling presentations that resonate with your buyers.

Time Management Planner

TIME MANAGEMENT PLANNER

PROJECT NAME :

DATE	DESCRIPTION	TIME IN	TIME OUT	TOTAL TIME

Sales professionals often juggle multiple tasks, and effective time management is crucial for success. This planner allows you to schedule your day, prioritize tasks, and ensure that you're dedicating enough time to high-impact activities. By using this planner, you can maximize your productivity and ensure that you're always working towards your goals.

The tools and resources provided in this appendix are designed to complement the knowledge and skills you've gained throughout the 31-day challenge. By incorporating these resources into your daily routine, you'll be better equipped to continue your journey towards sales mastery and sustained success in your career.

www.ingramcontent.com/pod-product-compliance
Lightning Source LLC
Chambersburg PA
CBHW070201230526
45471CB00002B/761